The Helvetic Reformation

The Helvetic Reformation

J. P. Whitney

WIPF & STOCK · Eugene, Oregon

Wipf and Stock Publishers
199 W 8th Ave, Suite 3
Eugene, OR 97401

The Helvetic Reformation
By Whitney, J. P.
ISBN 13: 978-1-5326-1606-8
Publication date 2/1/2017
Previously published by Cambridge University Press, 1934

THE HELVETIC REFORMATION.

The Helvetic Reformation, like the German, was the outcome of both the national history and the Renaissance. The history of Switzerland had been a record of free communities in town or country, more than holding their own under changing local dynasties and weakening imperial power. Gradually a sense of national unity emerges, but earlier local connexions are long retained. The Teutonic communities of Uri, Schwyz, and Unterwalden separately gain their independence in ways common enough elsewhere, and then become the centre of the later confederation. The lands around them are divided into two strongly marked parts—a Burgundian west, looking towards France, Burgundy, and Savoy, converted by Gallic or Roman missionaries, divided among many dynasties, and a Swabian or Alamannic east, richer in civilisation and democratic cities, converted by Irish missionaries, looking by the run of its valleys and the lie of its plains towards Germany. This division lasts through the Frankish Empire and through the Middle Ages, and is the most essential feature in Swiss history.

The growth of the early Habsburg power, following the extinction of the House of Zäringen (1218), at first threatened the freedom of the Swiss; the connexion of the Habsburg House with the Empire gave it an imperial claim to jurisdiction in addition to the varied local claims it already possessed, though at the same time it absorbed its energy in other and more important fields. The tendencies to union shown by the German Leagues operated also among the Swiss communities, and in the end gave rise to the Perpetual League of the three Forest Cantons, Schwyz, Uri, and Unterwalden (August, 1291), with simple provisions for maintaining their primitive liberty and regulating their mutual relations. The League concluded at Brunnen on December 13, 1315, after the great battle of Morgarten, added nothing essential, although it bound the members more closely together against a usurping lord. The accidents of Habsburg history and the varied grouping of the neighbouring Powers kept this early league alive and even caused it to grow: victories against the Habsburgs and afterwards against Burgundy confirmed its strength and increased its reputation. Soon cities with dependent villages under them, Luzern, Zurich, and Bern, joined the Confederates, and introduced divergent interests and policies. Around central Switzerland with its thirteen Cantons—those already mentioned, with Glarus, Zug, Freiburg, Solothurn, Basel, Schaffhausen, and Appenzell—there arose other leagues, the League of God's House among the subjects of the see of Chur, the Graubünden (or Grisons), and the League of the Ten Jurisdictions, differing in constitution and with histories of their own. In varying relations to the Confederation stood also allied States (the Valais, the town and Abbey of St Gallen, and others).

The Federal government not only gathered fresh members, but made conquests of its own: the Aargau (1415), partly divided between Bern and Zurich, partly, in the Free Bailiwicks, ruled jointly by the six Cantons (Zurich, Luzern, Schwyz, Unterwalden, Zug, and Glarus); the Thurgau, similarly ruled, but with special relations to Zurich. The government of these Common Lands was a difficult matter, as there was no Federal organisation beyond the Diet, to which the Cantons sent delegates. The Free Bailiwicks were administered by a Bailiff (*Landvogt*), appointed for two years by each of the six Cantons in turn. This defective system demanded perfect unity among the Confederates before it could work; and the chance of discord was greater because these Subject Lands lay between Zurich and Bern, and closed the path northwards from the Forest Cantons. To the south moreover conquests had been made towards Italy, and thus the Confederates were brought into touch with Italian as well as with German and more western politics.

Among the Confederates, Zurich (which joined them May, 1351) held a peculiar place. Favoured by Austria, and as an imperial city, Zurich had followed a distinct policy of its own which had at times led to war (for instance, 1442–50). What Bern, with its distinct aims and more aristocratic constitution, was to the west, Zurich, with its important gilds and widespread trade, was to the east. The Confederacy was again divided by the diversity of interests between rural and urban Cantons; moreover, city factions, as at Luzern, Zurich, and Bern, had looked to the Confederacy for help, and conversely civic disturbances could shake the Confederate League. The conquests from Austria, and the entanglement in the wars of France and Burgundy, and in those of Italy, involved the Confederacy in external relations out of all proportion to its constitutional growth. The problem of Federal organisation was handed down unsolved by the Middle Ages, together with conditions that made it difficult of solution.

Huldreich Zwingli was born on New Year's Day, 1484, at Wildhaus in the valley of Toggenburg. This district, after the extinction of its dynasty (1436), had been an object of strife between Zurich and Schwyz;

but in the end it had passed by purchase to the Abbey of St Gallen. The inhabitants of Wildhaus had gained the rights of electing their village bailiff and choosing their own village priest. Zwingli's father held the former, and his uncle Bartholomew the latter, office; when this uncle (1487) became rural dean and rector of Wesen on the Lake of Wallenstadt, the young boy, already destined for clerical life, went with him. His family was thus respected and versed in civil and ecclesiastical matters; on the mother's side, too, one uncle was Abbot of Fischingen, and another relative Abbot of Old St John's, near Wesen. In 1494 Zwingli was sent to Basel to be under Gregory Bünzli, and in 1498 to Bern, where his teacher was Heinrich Wölflin (Lupulus), then the most famous humanist in Switzerland. He was moved from Bern, lest the Dominicans should secure him as a novice, and he is next found at Vienna, where his classical bent was strengthened. In 1502 he returned to Basel where, in 1504, he graduated as Bachelor; the University was not then at its best, but the city was still a centre of Swiss life and of the trade in books; he became a teacher at St Martin's School, and thus his mind was early trained in the habit of instruction. In 1506 he was called to the charge of Glarus, an important town with three outlying hamlets, and was ordained priest at Constance.

The impulses forming his character had been simple: the democratic spirit of a self-governing village with traditions of its struggles—in 1490 he must have seen the Abbot of St Gallen appear with a small army to reduce his subjects to obedience; the training of the parish priest with a sense of responsibility (discharged as he even then significantly held mainly by preaching); the life of the village with its many activities of a smaller kind. But stronger than all these was his humanistic training, which at Glarus he had time to follow out. Traces of the current classical taste are seen in him to the end: one of these was his belief in the divine inspiration of Cato and other ancients with their high ideal of patriotism; hence, too, came his deep interest in the salvation of the great ancients who lived before Christ. But he was a humanist who never sought a patron.

Before he came to Glarus he had been under the influence of Thomas Wyttenbach (1505–6), a lecturer at Basel, from whom he had learnt the evils of Indulgences and the authority of the Bible. These crude ideas of reform were not however confined to Wyttenbach, and it was only in order to minimise his debt to Luther that Zwingli mentions this earlier indebtedness. But he had made closer acquaintance with Church abuses; for Heinrich Göldli, a Swiss of the Papal Guard and a trafficker in benefices, had bought the reversion of Glarus, and Zwingli had to pay him a pension of 100 *gulden* before entering upon his charge.

In classics Erasmus was his guide; good letters and sound theology were to go together; the spirit of the German Renaissance was to inspire theology; but of deep personal religion Zwingli at this stage was ignorant. That he never went to rest at night without having read a little in his master's works, as he said in a letter to the master himself, may not have been strictly true; but the dominant influence of Erasmus upon Zwingli, never overcome although combined with other influences, admits of no doubt. He may also have learnt from Erasmus something in the way of negation, such as a contempt for relics; something, too, he may have learnt from Pico della Mirandola, for whose sake he was once called a heretic at Basel; but from anti-papal tendencies he was quite free. From this young humanist—paradoxically combining a deep sense of responsibility with notable laxity in his moral life—no programme of reform was as yet to be looked for. His was a mind that moved gradually towards its fuller plans, and needed a fitting field wherein to work.

In 1513 he had again taken up the study of Greek, in which a little later Bombasius became his teacher; and he went to the New Testament itself rather than to any commentaries; the Fathers however attracted him, and it was at Glarus that he read Jerome (to whom Erasmus could not fail to send him), Augustine, Origen, Cyril, and Chrysostom. Of all these Augustine was his favourite—a fact to be noted in discussing his theology; but he considered the Greek Fathers to be more excellent in their Christology than were the Latin. Hebrew, possibly begun before, was studied later at Zurich in 1519 or 1520, but needed a renewed effort in 1522. He ever insisted upon the need of a learned clergy, and studied Holy Writ as he had learned to study the classical writers—a method which lent freshness to his teaching, but laid him open to a charge of irreverence.

Through his devotion to Erasmus and his friendship with Heinrich Loriti of Glarus (Glareanus) Zwingli gained an entry into the world of letters, which inherited the cosmopolitanism of the medieval universities, and which was now beginning to group itself around presses such as Froben's at Basel and Froschauer's at Zurich (1519). This was of importance, not only for his growing reputation, but also as bringing him into touch with wider interests. In his later years of diplomacy the habit of correspondence and the varied associations thus formed proved of use. Equally important too was the skill with which he drew around him younger men—some to find their goal in humanism, some in religious reform; in their after life and in their studies (mainly at Vienna) he followed them from afar and regularly wrote to them. Thus before he founded a school he had the scholars ready, and his name was a power among the younger men.

During these years at Glarus he became entangled in that system of wars and pensions which was the glory and the shame of his fatherland. The Italian wars brought not only much wealth to Switzerland, but also an increase of territory. To keep the Swiss as allies Louis XII had (1503) surrendered Bellinzona to them; when Massimiliano Sforza was made

Duke of Milan (1512) they received from him the Val Maggia, Locarno, and Lugano, while the Rhaetian League (the Grisons) gained the Valtelline. The Swiss Diets were besieged by agents of the Powers. A French party was to be found in every town, and a papalist anti-French party was created by Matthäus Schinner, Cardinal of Sion, in the service of Julius II. Zwingli's interest in politics was great; politics and patriotism inspired his earliest German poems,—the *Labyrinth*, and the *Fable of the Ox and the Beasts*; his position in Glarus made him a valuable ally for the papal party in a parish where the French were strong; it was therefore natural—although afterwards made a charge against him—that he should accept from the Pope a pension of 50 florins (1512 or 1513); and he was also (August 29, 1518) appointed acolyte chaplain. So far was he from being anti-papal that the Papacy was the one Power with which he held it right, even dutiful, to form alliances. Twice—but probably not thrice—he went to Italy as chaplain with the Glarus contingent; according to Bullinger he was present at Novara (June 6, 1513) and at Marignano (September 13-14, 1515); on the latter occasion his persuasion kept the Glarus men faithful to their service when others deserted to the French. Afterwards he indicates this as the period when he formed his well-known views upon the evils of mercenary service. The life of a mercenary—in camp or city—destroyed the simplicity endeared to Zwingli by the earlier Confederate history and classic models.

In 1515 the papal alliance came to an end: the terrible experience of Marignano on the one hand, and the acquisition of territory on the other, had made the Confederates desirous of peace, and (November 29, 1516) a permanent peace was made with France. Zwingli's opposition to this change of policy made his position at Glarus untenable, and he became people's priest (or vicar) at Einsiedeln (April 14, 1516), placing a vicar at Glarus. Einsiedeln, owing to its renown as a place of pilgrimage, combined the quiet of a monastic House with the traffic of a place of passage. Here he carried further his classical studies and increased his reputation as a preacher; he carefully trained himself in oratory by a study of the best classic models.

The personalities of the three great leaders, Erasmus, Luther (to whom Zwingli considered he was prior in his teaching), and Zwingli, were very different. Luther, with his monastic training, cared little for Catholic organisation; but he had a fervid personal experience and a strong love for doctrine. Erasmus combined piety and theological learning with much freedom of speech, tempered by regard for authority and a historic sense. Zwingli had from the first no regard for authority—which indeed presented itself at times in a guise hard to respect; he belonged to a country peculiarly weak in its ecclesiastical organisation and abounding in clerical abuses. But he had a deep regard for learning and a love of freedom, personal and intellectual.

He had no vivid perceptions of dogma recording the struggles of the soul. But he learnt from his varied parochial experience to realise keenly the relations between a pastor and his people. He had no deep philosophic basis for his opinions, and he was no framer of theories; he needed the touch of actual life to bring his powers to work, and he needed a field that suited him before he could form a definite policy. So far he was a keen Swiss patriot, with that love of the past that had formed the legend of Tell, a humanist, and a Reformer of the type of Erasmus, if indeed he was a Reformer at all.

If he was correct in his own view of his mental history, he took up an anti-papal stand from the first, and not, as Luther did, pressed by the course of argument. "The Papacy must fall," he said to Capito in 1517. But the humanists had inherited something of scholastic freedom in discussion, and to call the papal authority in question was no new thing in 1517. There was little significance in this expression of opinion from one who held a papal pension, and had done his best to secure help for the Papacy in what many of its friends condemned—its Italian wars and temporal policy.

After refusing one post at Winterthur, he received the offer of another, that of people's priest at the Great Minster of Zurich. His reputation as a preacher was in his favour; the new Provost of the Chapter—Felix Frei—had humanistic sympathies, and the political views, which had made him enemies at Glarus, were not against him here, for similar views had friends at Zurich; foreign pensions had been forbidden by the *Pensionbrief* of 1503, and met with warm opposition in the Chapter; the French alliance also was of less importance here. His appointment was preceded by much negotiation; there were rivals, and a story was brought up to his discredit which he could neither in the main deny, nor yet adequately defend; indeed, the tone of his defence showed a lack of moral sense. Finally the influence of his friends, especially of Myconius (Oswald Geisshüssler), schoolmaster at the Minster school, gained him the election (December 11, 1518), 17 out of a chapter of 24 voting for him. The office of people's priest or vicar at the Minster, thus gained, he kept until 1522; later he received a prebend after he had resigned his papal pension.

Zwingli had thus come to the proper field of his religious and political work. His development had so far been independent, not influenced even by Luther; and yet the movement begun by Zwingli owes much of its importance to that initiated by the German Reformer. Their likeness was the product of the time: their differences were not only doctrinal. Luther was no humanist, nor did his work lie in a Swiss city or in the Swiss Confederation. The special type of Protestantism presented to the world by Zwingli was due to his field of work being a city commonwealth with a peculiar history, political and ecclesiastical. But the ideas with which he started were the results of his humanism and of his previous work.

First among his ideas comes that of his prophetical office: he had gained his experience of life as a parish priest; his heart had gone into learning and education; these factors combined to form his vision of a prophet-pastor. From the Old Testament he took the notion of a prophet teaching morality, and not shrinking from politics where they had to be touched; but he added to this the ideal of instruction. He thus brought to his new work the loftiest conceptions of spiritual authority and responsibility. But his view left no room for other authority or for ecclesiastical superiors. The prophet was to do his work in the community,—not the community of the congregation regarded as part of a wider Church, but the political community in which he lived. Preaching—for which his life and training fitted him—was to be the means of teaching; it was well adapted for influencing a democracy and was characteristic of his system, where the pulpit superseded the altar, and where the intellectual element was large.

The relation of the prophet to his community was tinged by the influence of the Old Testament, and affected by the conditions of Swiss life. It was the prophet's work to teach, to inspire the magistracy; but it was theirs to carry out the policy. Thus he and they had to work together. This left large ecclesiastical powers to the community, and such the city had already claimed for itself; it gave wide scope to the personal influence of the pastor, both over the political assemblies and over the burgesses themselves. The acquisition of that influence, and the full use of it, were therefore essential to Zwingli's success.

Zurich had grown up around the Great Minster and the Minster of our Lady, foundations of Charles the Great and Ludwig the German respectively. The site was well adapted for trade, and, between the competing jurisdictions of the Abbess, the Provost of the Great Minster, and the Bailiff of the Emperor, a peculiarly free development was possible. There had been many contests between the city and its clergy. Arnold of Brescia, whose visit left traces, had sojourned there (1140-5); the liability of the clergy to pay taxes had been discussed and enforced. As a rule the monasteries were not only assessed for taxation, but subject to visitation by the State; and one of the few Federal documents that went into detail laid down the subjection of ecclesiastics to all ordinary jurisdiction (the *Pfaffenbrief* of 1370).

Swiss history—apart from legend—had been so far singularly poor in individual types. The most striking exception was that of Hans Waldmann, who had left a conspicuous mark on the constitution of Zurich. In 1483 he became Burgomaster, and for some years stood out as the leading statesman in Switzerland; foreign Powers gave him gifts and negotiated with him as with a prince. Though he was opposed by the aristocrats, he succeeded in carrying out a constitutional reform, excellent for the city, but stringent and oppressive for the surrounding villages.

Up to this time the *Constafel*, the original citizens, knights, merchants, and men of independent means, had been the leading element in the constitution. Rudolf Brun (1336) had placed the Gilds of handworkers, 13 in number, afterwards 12, alongside of the *Constafel*: their Masters became members of the smaller Council along with other Councillors, elected variously. At the head of the Constitution stood the Burgomaster, and for special purposes the Great Council of 200 (exactly 212) was called together. Waldmann, whose sympathies were with the Gilds, gave them more power in the constitution, and reduced the direct representation of the *Constafel* in the Smaller Council from 12 to 6. These civic regulations were confirmed even by his enemies after his execution; but discontent was caused by his strict enactments about trade and agriculture which weakened the country for the good of the city; the ill-will thus caused led to the riots preceding his death and left their mark behind. In the end the villages gained through the mediation of the other States an organisation (*Gemeinde*) of their own, through which they could act and consult with Zurich.

Waldmann claimed for the city the right to legislate for the Church, and to regulate the life and demeanour of ecclesiastics, and thus gave an impulse to the ecclesiastical independence of Zurich, already considerable. A document, dating from 1510 and often wrongly termed a Concordat, summed up the ecclesiastical powers claimed by Zurich and permitted to her by the Pope, anxious for such a useful ally. The diocesan divisions of Switzerland corresponded to no national limits and were included in different provinces—Constance and Chur under Mainz, Basel and Lausanne under Besançon, and Sion under Tarantaise, until freed by Leo X from its dependence. The Bishop of Constance, in whose diocese Zurich lay, was not well placed to assert his authority in this powerful city, and had seen many of his rights as to jurisdiction and appointments superseded.

When Zwingli went to Zurich, he therefore found a city democratic in its institutions (more so, for instance, than Bern), where a capable orator and man of affairs would be able to come to the front speedily; its history had made its relations with the Papacy and the Bishop mere matters of policy; the Church had as against the State little independence of its own, and there was no traditional dislike of change. For such a community he was well fitted: the political questions to which he had given most thought were those upon which opinion at Zurich was already divided; his power of speech, carefully trained and developed, could easily gain him power in a city with some 7000 burghers, and by his expositions on market-days he was able also to gain influence over the country people.

Zwingli found also in the press a helpful ally; the printer Froschauer was one of his closest adherents; his writings, which bear the mark of extempore utterance rather than of careful preparation, were often intended for the press, and spread through its channels of trade; letters could be sent and received through the same means, for the printer's house was a centre of news and communication: Froschauer, for instance, had a branch establishment at Frankfort and could circulate Zwingli's writings easily and carry his letters for him. The effect of Zwingli's works—hastily written for the most part, rarely classic in form or of permanent value for thought—was often immediate and great; he was a religious pamphleteer of learning, vigour, and experience.

In his private life there are few dates of importance. He was attacked by the plague (September, 1519), to meet which he had courageously returned from a holiday; but there are no reasons for regarding this illness as a religious crisis in his life. His marriage with Anne Reinhard, widow of Hans Meyer of Knonau, son of a distinguished family, took place (April 2, 1524) after a dubious connexion of some two years, and was hailed by some of his friends as a tardy though welcome act of courage. By the end of 1525 his Reformation at Zurich was in effect completed; and from that time onward his activity was either political or directed against Anabaptist enemies.

In February, 1519, the Franciscan Bernardin Samson, who had previously encountered Zwingli at Einsiedeln, reached Zurich to preach his Indulgence. Zwingli opposed him at once and with success; the Bishop of Constance forbade the clergy of the diocese to admit Samson into their churches; the Council of Zurich forbade his entry into the city. But Zwingli and Luther met with very different treatment: Samson was ordered by the Pope himself not to vex the authorities of Zurich, and rather than do so to depart; no breach between the Papacy and Zwingli resulted; a monk who wished to print abuse of him was checked by both Legate and Bishop. The first sign of anti-papal feeling upon his part comes after the Imperial election (January–June, 1519). The papal policy in that matter was too shifty to commend itself to Zwingli's honest and outspoken nature, and moreover he wished the Swiss to stand aloof.

But the Lutheran drama had by this time come to a crisis, and following the advice of friends, Beatus Rhenanus among them, Zwingli had interested himself in Luther's fate; after the Leipzig disputation he hailed him as "David" and "Hercules," and exerted himself to delay the publication of the Papal Bull against him. At this time too he read Hus' work *On the Church*, which is practically a new edition of Wiclif's *De Ecclesia*, and contains many of the doctrines—such as those touching the papal power, and the civil right to control the Church—afterwards taught by Zwingli.

The question how far Zwingli was indebted to Luther has been much discussed. Like Luther, he had been called a heretic after his opposition to Samson. To him as to others the name Lutheran was carelessly given. His private Biblical annotations show new doctrinal tendencies after 1522, when he had undoubtedly read Luther's works. But the assumption that he owed his views to Luther always roused his indignation, and a common Pauline element fully explains the likeness of their opinions, slight as it is. Zwingli tried to clear himself from the charge of imitation, and claimed for himself originality. In doing so he was justified, though his treatment of the charge shows some petulance and self-satisfaction. But it is too much to say that the bold stand made by Luther and the whole set of problems he raised had no effect upon Zwingli's mind and did nothing to direct his activity into new channels. Their original impulses, however, were very different, and their several treatment of Indulgences illustrates the difference. To Luther the question presented itself as a mistaken doctrine which struck at the root of religion; to Zwingli it was more a practical abuse, an encroachment of the Church upon the individual life.

The divergence of Zwingli from Erasmus and its occasion are also instructive. Hutten, in his energy and contempt for tradition, his licence and disregard of morality, had little in common with Erasmus on the one hand or with Luther on the other, although his love of learning and width of outlook joined him to both. Before his death, however, in August, 1523, a quarrel with Erasmus brought out the fundamental opposition between them. Zwingli, linked to Erasmus by early indebtedness and a scholar's reverence, had yet more in common with Hutten; and when the dying outcast, disowned by the calmer souls, reached Zurich, Zwingli befriended him; he did this, not from mere human sympathy, but also from the feeling of a common cause against the old society and the old traditions. But his action caused a breach between him and Erasmus, and with Glareanus also, "the shadow of Erasmus." This marks a certain separation of Zwingli from the aims of the humanist circles in which he had hitherto lived; for Basel and Einsiedeln, unlike Luzern, were both centres of learning.

In his sermons Zwingli, who was both outspoken and effective, attacked monasticism and the doctrines of Purgatory and the Invocation of Saints. But the first conflict took place when he attacked the principle of tithes. In a Latin sermon preached before the Chapter, he maintained that tithes had no foundation in the Divine Law, and should be voluntary. The Provost urged him in vain to recant, and not to furnish arms for the laity to use against the clergy (early in 1520). The same year a simplification of the breviary for the Minster was prepared and introduced (June 27, 1520)—a change arising out of Zwingli's earlier liturgical studies, and showing that the majority of the Chapter was on his side.

Religious parties were already forming themselves around him. He met with opposition both from the conservatives in the Chapter (including Conrad Hoffman, who had supported his election) and from the monks. The excitement raised was shown by a decree of 1520, ordering priests in town and country to preach conformably to the Gospels and Epistles and according to the guidance of the Holy Spirit and the

Bible, but to keep silence upon human innovations. This decree, proceeding not from the Bishop but from the civil rulers, and taking the Bible as a standard, exhibited two characteristics of the Zwinglian position.

The political events of these years were decisive for Zwingli and for Zurich. The French, at a Diet held at Luzern (May 5, 1521), strove to get support from the Confederates. Pensions had already done much harm to social and political life; the mercenary soldiers, whether abroad selling their lives for gold, or at home spending it in riot, were an injury to the State. The ostentatious display of wealth made by the French envoys, both in the Imperial election and now in their search for an alliance, emphasised the dangers of mercenary service. Zwingli, together with the Burgomaster Marcus Röust, opposed the French alliance; the Diet, however, made a treaty with Francis I by which he might enlist troops up to 16,000 under leaders of his own choice. The Bernese statesman Albrecht von Stein came to Zurich to secure its approval; for the city with its villages could raise an army of 10,000. But, stimulated by sermons of passionate patriotism from Zwingli, reminding them again and again of their hard-bought freedom and traditional simplicity, the Zurich Council rejected the French alliance. The Council of the Two Hundred answered to the Diet, that they would keep to their old leagues, and would have nothing to do with Princes, pensions, and foreign alliances; and the Pension decree which forbade the receipt of any alien gifts was to be sworn to by all the citizens twice a year. But the loss of wealth, the separation from the other Cantons, and the comparative stagnation of neutral life soon caused discontent in the Corinth of Switzerland; and Zwingli had to bear many reproaches. About this time he resigned his papal pension from conscientious scruples, but soon after received a canonry in the Minster with a prebend of 70 *gulden*; this benefice gave him the franchise, and from this time his political importance grew. He was now the centre of a growing group; Berthold Haller at Bern, Vadian (von Watt), the gifted Burgomaster of St Gallen, and others; the humanistic brotherhood was passing into a Reforming society, and was soon to be used as a diplomatic power.

Zwingli's defection from the Papacy was now only a matter of time. An incident often assigned as its cause was even more important for Zurich than for him. The Pope asked for a force to be used only for the defence of his States, not against the French or other Swiss. Zurich, which sent him half his body-guard, was the place where he sought it. Zwingli, who had once before supported a papal application, now opposed it. But a force of 6000 set out (September 16, 1521) and was in the end sent to Milan. The Council indignantly recalled it; but some of the soldiers followed Cardinal Schinner, and narrowly escaped a conflict with the Swiss mercenaries of France. To make things worse, their pay was withheld even after their return. The Council, supported by popular feeling, now forbade all foreign service (January 11, 1522).

This same year, the question of Lenten observance began the Zwinglian Reformation. Some of Zwingli's followers did not share his willingness to wait for the action of the magistracy. The printer Froschauer and others ate meat publicly, in the presence of Leo Jud and Zwingli himself. They could justify themselves by his teaching that nothing not commanded by Scripture was binding upon Christians, and he undertook their defence. His sermon *On the Choice or Freedom of Food* was preached now (March 30, 1522) and afterwards printed, as were many of his sermons delivered about this time. He advocated freedom for the individual, upon whom lay the responsibility to act without scandal.

The civic authorities made a compromise: no distinction was drawn, they said, by the New Testament between kinds of food; but for the sake of peace the old rule should be kept until changed by authority, and the people's priests were to check the people from any breach of this ruling. The disregard of custom and authority shown by the decree and the act leading to it could not be overlooked; and the Bishop of Constance sent a commission, consisting of his Suffragan (Melchior Wattli) and two others, to settle the matter. The commissioners laid their views before the priests and the Smaller Council, and commanded them to observe existing customs (April 7, 1522). Before the Great Council Zwingli answered the Suffragan's arguments, and the debate really turned upon Church authority and custom as against individual freedom. At its close the Council repeated its old decree, pending a settlement by the Bishop of Constance, which they begged him to make according to the law of Christ. This was a practical abrogation of episcopal power, for the Bishop's standing was clear. The Zwinglian Reformation, therefore, begins as an ecclesiastical revolution, founded on action rather than doctrine, by which a city freed itself from outward control and organised itself afresh.

His learned friend Johann Faber, the Vicar-General of Constance, afterwards an Aulic Councillor and Bishop of Vienna, had just returned from a visit to Rome (May, 1522) and thenceforth led the opposition against Zwingli. So early as 1519 the latter had marked him as one from whom, although a humanist, the Gospel had little to hope. Zwingli's literary work at this time recalls that of Wiclif in the years before his death; his *Archeteles*—a full statement of his position—was written in haste and appeared now (August 22, 1522). On reading it Erasmus begged him to be more cautious and to act with others; Œcolampadius also urged restraint. The same year (July 2) ten priests joined Zwingli in a petition to the Bishop to allow clerical marriage, wherein the wish for innovation was as distinct as the picture of existing morals was dark. There can be no doubt that the priests in Switzerland, owing partly to the disorganisation of episcopal rule and partly to the isolation of their parishes, had a low standard of life; of this there is ample evidence from both episcopal and Reforming documents. A like request made to the Federal Diet (July 13) was accompanied by a repudiation of the names Lutheran and Hussites. These requests had no result beyond making clear the position of those who preferred them.

At Zurich repeated troubles with the monks, and disturbances during Zwingli's sermons, made it necessary for the Burgomaster to restore order. His decree—this time coupled with no appeal to the Bishop— was that the pure Word of God must be preached, and the Scholastics (a term loosely used for teachers held to be old-fashioned) left alone. A Chapter (August 15) of the country clergymen came to the same decision. Thus backed by civic and clerical authority, Zwingli held himself free. The Bible—as interpreted by the responsible "Bishop" (so he terms all pastors and indeed in one place all humanists)—was to be the sole guide of faith. City and country, pastors and magistrates were combined into a stronghold of Reform. The system thus begun may be described on the one side as individualistic and on the other as civic. The appeal to the Scriptures alone was individualistic, due to humanism without prepossession; the civic element was due to the circumstances of Zurich.

In a federal republic accustomed to Diets a Public Disputation— suggested in *Archeteles*—seemed a likely way to settle controversies. It recalled at once University exercises and General Councils, it was at once learned and democratic. Such an assembly was called at the end of the year, and met in Zurich (January 29, 1523). The invitation to this Disputation shows the Great Council for the first time definitely on Zwingli's side; and each subsequent stage of the Swiss Reformation was marked by a similar encounter. Zwingli had resigned his parochial charge, but had been allowed by the Council the use of the pulpit. In the Disputation he and his doctrine were the central points of debate. To regulate the Disputation he had drawn up 67 theses.

The fundamental conception of the doctrine here set forth was that of the Church as a democratic body of all Christians, each in open communication with God independently of externals or means of grace, guided by the study of Scripture and the illumination of God's Spirit. To this conception the republicanism of letters and of Switzerland had each contributed something. Starting from this assumption, the Theses place the Gospel alone as the basis of truth and the secular authority as the governor of the organisation; they deny the power of Pope and hierarchy, the sacrifice in the Mass, the Invocation of Saints, Purgatory, times of fasting, and clerical celibacy.

About 600 were present at the Disputation, including representatives of the Bishop with Faber among them; Schaffhausen, however, was the only Canton which sent deputies. Faber urged the postponement of a decision until the expected General Council met; but Zwingli's reply was that the Word of God was the sole authority, and competent scholars could interpret it, so that there was no need of a Council's decision. When the audience met after dinner, the Burgomaster Röust, who presided, declared in the name of the Council that Zwingli had not been convicted of heresy, and therefore ordered that he should go on preaching the Holy Gospel with the Holy Spirit's help. Zurich was thus committed to Zwingli, and the importance of the decision was shown by Faber's printing his own account of what took place as a correction of the Zurich account. The First Disputation marks Zwingli's control of the city as established, and their joint complete and open rupture with the past.

Zwingli was now sure of his ground and could proceed more rapidly: his literary activity was accompanied by practical changes. Leo Jud had translated the Baptismal Office into German and used it (August 10, 1523). A committee was appointed to deal with the Minster Chapter, for which a new constitution was issued (September 29, 1523). Fees for Baptism and Burial were abolished; holders of Minster offices were to discharge their duties to the utmost of their health and strength; as they died off, their places were to be left unfilled (unless chaplains were needed), and the income was to be applied to other purposes. The Chapter's fall was not undeserved; for, though there were some excellent members, it had become a refuge for men of good family and poor education. The Bible was to be read by the Minster clergy publicly an hour a day in Hebrew, Greek and Latin, with explanations; free lectures and fit lodgings were provided for candidates for the ministry, so that they need no longer go abroad. The public lectures were the origin of the later "prophesying." In this scheme of teaching Zwingli had able helpers in Leo Jud, people's priest at All Saints (1523), and Myconius, now (1524) at the Minster school. Zwingli remained faithful to the principles of Erasmus, and never fell into the easy error of underestimating education as compared with spiritual zeal. The educational scheme was completed for Zurich itself, after the dissolution of the monasteries which followed in December, 1524. What remained of the Chapter's income when education had been provided for, went to the poor and the aged; in his poor-laws, as in all his social legislation, Zwingli showed a clear and almost modern appreciation of needs and methods, notably in his discouragement of mendicancy and use of careful enquiry.

The literary side of Zwingli's work in this stage was the *Auslegung und Begründung der Schlussreden*, an unsystematic explanation of the Theses for the Disputation. The work, which was preceded by a letter to the Council and people of Glarus, was a full and in parts lengthy exposition of the Theses; written in German, it was "a farrago of all the opinions which are controverted to-day." The explanations of the Theses upon the Papacy and the Mass are especially long, which is noteworthy, as Zwingli had as yet not attacked the Mass in practice.

1523]   *Doctrine and observances.—The Anabaptists.*   15

This work, written night and day amid the expectation of his friends, and incidentally discussing his relations with Luther, may be held to contain the full programme of the Helvetic Reformation (July 14, 1523). Not only did he dislike to be called Lutheran, but on some points, such as Purgatory, Confession, and Invocation of Saints, he differs from Luther. Against the monks he inveighs strongly: all monasteries ought to be turned into hospitals. The Reformation in Switzerland made most way where there were many monasteries, and least where there were none; the differences that arose between the larger Houses and their tenants made the latter more eager to embrace Protestantism. And the secularisation of the monasteries—here laid down as desirable—was a very practical part of the Swiss Reformation: the peasants in some parts undoubtedly looked for profit from the dissolution. Zwingli also explains his method of dealing with doctrine; the Invocation of Saints he had let remain until the populace should have learnt to do without it and worship Christ alone. Confirmation and Extreme Unction he would retain as rites, not as Sacraments; but Auricular Confession, pictures, and music, should be banished from churches.

Zwingli held that it was his part to teach, but that to make changes belonged to the civic authority. But his teaching had led some of his followers to act without waiting for the civic rulers; pictures and images were torn down both in town and country. After much discussion the question came before the Great Council, which suspended judgment until a second Disputation should be held. This took place on October 26, 1523. The Bishops and the other Cantons were invited, but the Bishops did not come; 800 persons, 350 of them ecclesiastics, were present; this time St Gallen as well as Schaffhausen was represented; Luzern and Obwalden angrily refused the invitation. The first day's debate was upon images and pictures, which Zwingli held forbidden in all cases; some urged delay, but the final decision was that idols and pictures should be removed, but without a breach of the peace; those who had already broken the peace were to be pardoned as a rule, but a leader, Nicholas Hottinger, was afterwards banished for two years. On the second day the Mass was discussed; Zwingli had prepared Theses according to which the Mass was no sacrifice and had been surrounded by abuses. But the appearance in this Disputation of the Anabaptists, an organised radical party basing their views upon his teaching, and yet going beyond him in action, hampered him greatly and made the magistracy cautious.

At the Disputation Zwingli noted in a formal way that the ecclesiastical authorities had done nothing; this was true, although the Bishop of Constance had in a dignified note asserted his constitutional position; he could not appear, and he begged them to exercise restraint. But the civil authorities were now, in Zwingli's view and in their own, called upon to act. A commission of eight members of the two

Councils and six ecclesiastics was named to discuss what steps should be taken. Until a settlement the clergy were to be instructed by an epistle, which Zwingli was asked to write; preachers were also sent out; Wolfgang Joner, Abbot of Kappel, who had lately called the younger Bullinger to his help, together with others, visited the Canton; Zwingli himself went in the direction of the Thurgau. The Second Disputation, wherein discussion turned solely on the interpretation of the Scriptures, marks a fresh stage in the Reformation, even apart from the appearance of the Anabaptists. The *Short Introduction to Christian Doctrine* (*Eine kurze christliche Inleitung*) is its literary monument.

The Reformation was now no longer a purely civic affair. From the first the Catholic Cantons had been indisposed to treat it as such; among people of simple minds and with an unformed Federal system religious innovation and religious discord put a heavy strain both upon Federal action and other bonds of union. The Federal Diet at Baden (September 30, 1523) had threatened all innovators with punishment, and Luzern in particular had shown by its action the strength of its feelings. The Reformation had thus already divided the Confederation, and no Diet had been held at Zurich since March, 1522; the union of the Cantons before this time had, however, been so loose that it is easy to overestimate the retrograde effects of the Reformation.

The *Introduction*, written in fourteen days, was circulated in November, 1523, and was intended for the clergy, not the public. It started from an explanation of the relations between the Law and the Gospel, passing on to an application to present needs, the question of images, and that of the Mass. Throughout the Canton priests here and there ceased to say mass; when Conrad Hoffman and the Catholics of the Chapter complained, the Council, advised by the parish priests, forbade them to speak or act against what had been settled, under pain of loss of their benefices and banishment; at Whitsuntide a full settlement should be made (January, 1524). A further appeal from the Catholic Cantons to abstain from innovations (February 25, 1524) only called forth the answer that they would observe the Federal League, but could not yield in matters of conscience (March 21). For Christmas Day, 1523, Zwingli had announced an administration in both kinds at the Cathedral, and the substitution of a sermon for the daily mass. The Council, however, decreed that until Whitsuntide old Mass and new Administration should continue side by side. Images and crucifixes—the use of which had been quietly checked for some time—were on no account to be carried about. The exact form of the substitute for the Mass was to be settled at a fresh Disputation (December 19, 1523).

When Whitsuntide came (May 15, 1524) the Council resolved to act on its own authority without waiting for the Bishop. The committee appointed in 1523 suggested the removal of pictures and images by legally named authorities at the wish of each community, and Zwingli

1524-5] *Abolition of the Mass and the monasteries.* 17

urged the replacing of the early Mass by a sermon and the Lord's Supper. The committee, however, did not altogether follow him as to the Mass; this was left in use, but the images were removed. The tardy intervention of the Bishop, defending the Mass and images, was disregarded. This decision was adopted by both Councils and sent round to the bailiffs in the country for execution (June–July). The majority of a village, however, could decide to keep or remove images as they pleased. Removal was to be carried out by the pastor and responsible men; the use of organs, the passing bell, and extreme unction were also abolished. A reply to the Bishop was composed by Zwingli, who was now all-powerful, and approved by the Council. The section on the Mass is Zwingli's first complete statement of his views, which he was now developing. He carried on a controversy, partly as to this subject, with Jerome Emser of Leipzig, who had attacked Luther for his alteration of the Canon; in his *Antibolon* (August 18) in answer to this opponent, in an *Apology* addressed to Diebold Geroldseck (October 9, 1523), in his *De Canone Missae Epichiresis* (1523), in his *Subsidium sive Coronis de Eucharistia* (1525), and in his *De Vera et Falsa Religione* (1525) Zwingli dealt with this central point. Negatively, he repudiated all sacramental efficacy, and reduced the rite to a mere sign (*nuda signa*): positively, he laid great stress—notably in his reply to Emser—upon its aspect as a feast and a corporate act; it was therefore social, not merely individual in its importance.

The Mass at Zurich was abolished in April, 1525, but the religious Houses had been previously suppressed; the monks who did not return to the world were placed together in the Franciscan monastery; the convent of the Minster of our Lady (December 4, 1524) and the Chapter of the Great Minster (December 20) gave up their possessions to the city; the monasteries throughout the Canton followed. The incomes were devoted to education or the poor; a *gymnasium*, for instance, was endowed with the funds of the Great Minster, and Zwingli himself became rector of the Carolinum (April 14, 1525) as the united scholastic foundations were called. His scheme of graduated studies leading up to the ministry was adequate and well thought out. By a development of the plan of Biblical instruction begun in 1523 the prophesyings or expositions took the place of the choir services, while the linguistic instruction was extended (July 19, 1525). When a Synodal organisation (September 23, 1527) and Church Courts (*Stillstände*) for discipline and marriage-cases were set up (May 10, 1525), the Reformation upon its constructive as well as its destructive side was completed. As a purely civic organisation even in its details it was systematic and orderly: a register of baptisms, for instance, was begun in 1526 for the city and afterwards extended to the Canton. Of the elaborate system thus established Zwingli was the "Bishop" and the soul.

It seems strange to find the Council at this date (August 19, 1524) writing to the Pope that they were unable to stop the course of change, even had they wished, owing to the strength of popular opinion. The Pope's reply was conciliatory, and prolonged negotiations took place (1525–6); the city trying to obtain the arrears of its military pay, and Clement VII seeking to keep the city firm in its old alliance. In no respect were the positions of Luther and of Zwingli more contrasted than in the treatment they received from the Papacy; and the cause of this was the papal hope of help from Zurich.

The civic position of Zwingli was now significant. Theoretically he might consider the congregation the ecclesiastical power, but in practice the community acted. He had realised his conception of the prophet guiding the community; nay more, he was, as Salat says, "Burgomaster, secretary, and Council in one." First the Great Council, the democratic body, had been won, then the Smaller Council, and finally events gave Zwingli even further power. Marcus Röust and Felix Schmid, the experienced Burgomasters, had died (1524); Joachim am Grüt, Zwingli's opponent in the debates upon the Mass (1525), had been dismissed from his office of city clerk (end of 1525). Zwingli was the sole leader left. At a threatening crisis (November 20, 1524) the Burgomaster and the chief Gild-master received authority to settle pressing business privately with the help of trusty men. This is the first appearance of the Privy Council in and through which Zwingli afterwards worked, and to which foreign affairs were mainly entrusted. The experience of the Peasants' War (1524–5) inclined Zwingli to a body less democratic than a large assembly, and his policy often required secresy. Through this body, the *Heimliche Rath*, or the Privy Six, which became permanent in 1529, Zwingli exerted his influence. The Council itself was "purged" by the exclusion of those opposed to him (December 9, 1528), who were found chiefly among the nobles. The numbers representing the *Constafel* in the two Councils were reduced, from 6 to 3, and from 18 to 12, respectively (1529). Thus beyond the Protestant democracy and the two Councils stood the commanding personality of Zwingli, working through and upon each of them, but above them all, through the Privy Six.

Zwingli had been so gently treated by the Pope, and his career had been so fortunate, that his conflict with the Anabaptists might well seem to him the hardest struggle undergone by him. The leaders of that party had been among those who, by eating flesh in Lent, began the breach with episcopacy. They and their followers pulled down crucifixes before the State had legalised such acts; but they could appeal to Zwingli's teaching. They first appear as a distinct party in the Second Disputation (October, 1523). Conrad Grebel—son of Jacob Grebel, executed November, 1526, for treason—and Felix Manz, both men of influential families and with private grudges against Zwingli, were leaders of this radical party in the city; outside the city were other local centres—Zolliken, Wyteken, and Höngg. The dislike of tithes—

so loudly expressed in the Peasants' Revolt—was shared by many Anabaptists; and at Grüningen, a centre where this economic side of the Anabaptist movement showed itself, it united with that of the peasants. Zwingli himself was averse from levying the small tithes upon vegetables and fruit; he held further that tithes had merely legal, but no Scriptural, warrant. The Council, however, disagreed with him, and tithes were maintained.

At first the movement was indigenous; but late in 1524 Münzer came to Waldshut (N.W. of Zurich), and Carlstadt to Zurich itself; some German Anabaptists from St Gallen also worked in Zurich territory; these influences from outside intensified the movement and organised it. But it was more a radical than a doctrinal movement; and hence Zwingli, jealous for the unity of his new organisation and yet largely in sympathy with their views, appealed to the Anabaptists in vain not to found a separate body. When they did so, a public Disputation with them, the first of several, was arranged (January 17–18, 1525), and it was followed by a decree that all unbaptised children must be baptised within a week, or their parents would be banished. Some of the leaders were imprisoned; and with these Zwingli held private and repeated discussions.

Inasmuch as this new society rejected the authority of magistrates and pastors alike, the Council by severe punishment tried to suppress the movement. Manz was put to death by drowning (January 7, 1527), and the foreign leaders were banished, most of them to meet violent deaths later and elsewhere. In spite of Zwingli's severity against them, due to his resentment as a rejected leader, whom they had come to hate as "the false prophet," their small congregations continued to exist. Their energy afterwards found vent in needed criticism of clerical life; and the Synod of Easter, 1528, had for one of its objects a tightening of clerical discipline which might meet the objections and gain over the objectors.

After the final removal of the Mass the radicals turned to social matters, and, especially at Grüningen, attacked the tithes. An agitation against tithes and the monasteries had to a great extent common objects with the Zwinglians; the houses of Rüti and Bubikon were attacked by rioters; and a popular assembly at Töss (June 5, 1525) caused great fear. The defeat of the Peasants' Revolt in Germany made the allied movement easier to deal with in Switzerland, and Zwingli's negotiations, together with public disputations, resulted in a settlement. Tithes remained, but personal servitude, where the ownership of the State was concerned, was done away with. The villagers of the lake communes were henceforth regarded as citizens of the town. The general result here as in Germany was to arouse a dread of change; and outside Zurich Zwingli's teaching was greatly blamed as an exciting cause. Incidentally, the vain attempt of Ulrich of Württemberg to regain his duchy by the help of the peasants and Swiss mercenaries had made the governments at Ensisheim and Innsbruck suspicious of Switzerland. The grievances of the peasants, intensified by the effect of the Reformation upon the public lands, remained unredressed, and, a century later, led to the Peasants' War (1653). Few chapters in the history of federalism are more instructive than this failure on the part of a democratic federation to govern its conquests or to respect their liberties.

The Reformation had brought a new cause of division into the Confederacy. Religious disunion—save in the occasional form of heresy—was an unlooked-for thing, and the Federal authority scarcely knew how to treat it. The Forest Cantons were keen enemies of change; they regarded the Zurich innovations as threatening to themselves. On the other hand Zurich naturally regarded herself as free to make what changes she wished. This difficulty would have strained Federal relations, especially where much of Church government had been already taken over by the civil power; but it might have been overcome. When Zurich—disregarding the principle of government by the majority of the Cantons—pushed religious change into the Subject Lands the difficulty was increased. The frequent division of the higher and lower jurisdiction between the Confederates and a single Canton gave rise to the further question: under which jurisdiction came religious offences? The majority of the Cantons governing the Subject Lands were Catholic; Zurich in many places held the lower jurisdiction. As early as November, 1522, the Federal Diet ordered the bailiffs in the Subject Lands to bring before them the priests who spoke against the faith, thus claiming religious offences for the higher jurisdiction. But these beginnings of discord in the Federation were bound up with the beginnings of a local reformation upon Catholic lines.

The Bishop of Constance, like his brother-Bishop Christopher von Uttenheim of Basel, had tried to improve his diocese, as his pastoral letter of 1517 shows. With these efforts there was widespread sympathy, and when the three Bishops of Basel, Lausanne, and Constance complained to the Diet at Luzern (January 26, 1524) of the disturbed state of things in their dioceses, the Diet not only (as already noted) sent an embassy to Zurich urging caution, but proposed to undertake a reformation on the lines of unity, admitting that abuses ought to be redressed. Exactions, traffic in benefices, Indulgences were condemned; the Diet would consult with Zurich as to the best means of shaking off the yoke which the injustice of Popes, Cardinals, and prelates had laid upon the Swiss people. But this reformation was to be undertaken by the State, and the Federal Diet was to be the ruling authority. Nothing could better prove the ecclesiastical anarchy into which Switzerland had fallen, and the chance that a reforming Papacy would have had of preserving unity and yet securing progress. Luzern, whence these proposals came, was afterwards a centre of the Counter-Reformation.

They were rejected by Zurich, but resulted in the Disputation at Baden (May-June, 1526). Zwingli, however, it was easy to see, cared little for unity or peace, compared with the carrying out of his own far-reaching plans.

At Beckenried, April 8, 1524, the Five Cantons, Luzern, Uri, Schwyz, Unterwalden, and Zug, formed a separate league to suppress all Hussite, Lutheran, or Zwinglian errors. A further remonstrance was made to Zurich by all the Cantons except Schaffhausen and Appenzell, and the intention of not sitting in Diet along with Zurich was declared (July 16, 1524). The Mass, pictures, images, and fasting were pronounced binding upon all Swiss. Zurich on the other hand declared religion to be a purely cantonal matter. This was a question hard to settle, with no precedents to refer to. Zurich, however, put itself in the wrong by its action in the Thurgau, where it held the lower jurisdiction, exercised through its bailiffs. Preachers, for the most part connected with Zwingli, had worked their way here—such as Oechsli (an old Einsiedeln friend of his) at Burg. When Oechsli was seized by the Federal officer who exercised the higher jurisdiction, his friends and parishioners gathered to rescue him (July 17, 1524): afterwards in a riotous mob they proceeded to the Carthusian monastery of Ittingen, and set it on fire. At Stammheim and Stein images were destroyed. The seizure of the leaders—three of whom were executed at Baden—embittered Zurich; but the other Cantons in their turn blamed its encouragement of the preachers.

Six Cantons (Luzern, Uri, Unterwalden, Schwyz, Zug, and Freiburg) now threatened to break the league; but Bern was inclined to support the independence of the Cantons, upon the principle *cujus regio, ejus religio*. At a Diet at Zug it was proposed to raise the country districts against Zurich on account of her destruction of images, but to this step Bern and Solothurn objected. Zurich had, however, made sure of the loyalty of her subjects in the religious changes, just as she referred to them the French alliance and the demands of the peasants. But the Cantons were now divided into hostile factions; and outside lay Austria, embittered by the help sent from Zurich to a rising at Waldshut and Swiss support of Duke Ulrich.

At the end of 1524 Zwingli, always fertile in suggestions and skilful in expression, came forward with a remarkable plan. Zurich was to strengthen herself in military equipment—her reputation for military strength was great; she was to seek alliances with France and Savoy; to promise St Gallen and the Thurgau the property of the monasteries in their territory as a price for their support; and to raise Tyrol against Austria. It is clear that Zwingli's range was extending: it was now that he entered into relations with Duke Ulrich; he now also took the religious movement in his old home, Toggenburg, under his care, and the Reformation was soon fully under way (1524-5).

The disaster of Pavia (February 24, 1525) wrought some change in Federal feeling; the loss of 5000 Swiss, followed by the retreat of the remainder, made the French alliance less popular; people freely cursed the French, pensions, and subsidies. Thus, Zwingli's old policy of doing away with mercenary service was recommended; but he had now departed from his former dislike of alliances. An alliance with France was soon one of his dearest hopes; his work at Zurich was safe; to make Protestantism in the Common Lands equally safe, and afterwards to gain freedom for his preachers in the Catholic Cantons, were now the objects of his policy. To carry such a policy into effect foreign alliances were needed. But nearer than France lay southern Germany, the cities of which were in many ways more like Zurich than was Bern, and here his doctrines made rapid way. These cities were naturally inclined to an organisation of religion that was at once civic and democratic; Strassburg—with its many subject villages—was a mediator by position and interest; the new diplomatists were the preachers, with something of Zwingli's influence in their respective cities, and many of them in constant correspondence with him. The decentralising of influences which had once centred in Rome or in the greater ecclesiastical Courts; the substitution of pastors and dogmatic leaders for Cardinals and Legates—these are leading features of Reformation politics. Thus the main interest of Zwingli's letters in the following years is political and diplomatic. His object was to give Zurich a great dominion such as she had sought and lost in the old Zurich war, to make her the *Vorort*, no longer of eastern Switzerland only, but of a new Confederacy reaching into the Empire and holding at bay the Emperor (of whom he wished to see the world well rid). But this dominion was to be based upon a common religion.

As the forces of religious change drew together, so did the forces of conservatism. Archduke Ferdinand had gathered the leading Catholic States (June, 1524) at Ratisbon; to them, as to the Diet at Luzern, the suppression of heresy seemed the most urgent duty; the minor ecclesiastical reforms secured from the Legate Campeggio fell far short of the Swiss plan of reform. Faber had been at this conference; in 1526 he became an imperial Councillor, and now he began to organise the Catholic party in Switzerland. For this purpose a Disputation was suggested at Baden (January 15, 1526); John Mayer of Eck—a many-sided and able man—was eager to meet Zwingli. But the latter at first declined to meet him anywhere save at Zurich; and afterwards, when Zwingli was ready to go to St Gallen or Schaffhausen, the Zurich Council refused him leave for the journey. When the meeting took place at Baden (May 21—June 18, 1526), he was therefore not present, and Œcolampadius from Basel had to take his place. But the most elaborate arrangements were made for sending him daily reports and receiving his advice. Eck, with his Theses, played the part that Zwingli had played at Zurich, and in the opinion of the majority (82 to

20) played it well. The reputation of the victory greatly strengthened the Catholic party.

But Zurich was now no longer the sole centre of Reform. At Schaffhausen, Hofmeister, at Biel, Wyttenbach, Zwingli's old teacher at Basel, were preaching freely. In Basel Capito's work (1512–20) was more than carried on by Œcolampadius, now (February, 1525) minister at St Martin's. Bern, the most important of all the cities, was, in religion as in politics, inclined to a policy of its own. Political power was here in the hands of the aristocracy, the gilds being politically unimportant; Berthold Haller and Sebastian Meier by their preaching shared the work of the painter-dramatist Nicholas Manuel, to whom some ascribe the direction of Bernese policy, until his death in 1530. Free preaching, if in accord with God's Word, was allowed, but innovations were forbidden; pictures, fasting, and other points disputed elsewhere were left untouched; but heretical books were prohibited (June 15, 1523; November 22, 1524). The magistracy, however, claimed the right to punish priests disregarding these decrees; the monasteries were placed under civic control, and clerical incomes were regulated. But the power of the preachers grew; and at Easter, 1527, both the Great and the Small Council had Protestant majorities. A decree maintaining the old worship for the present with a speedy prospect of change was passed; but some priests here as elsewhere anticipated the change. Political interests moved Bern in the same direction. Although disturbed by the Peasants' War, Bern was still unwilling to put pressure upon Zurich; and towards the end of 1526, through fear of Austria, drew nearer to her. Bern, Zurich, Basel, Glarus, and Appenzell did not share the desire of the Catholic Cantons to base their Federal union upon a common belief, but wished to found it only upon common interests.

The Bernese authorities decided, like Zurich, to hold a Disputation to which the Bishops and delegates from the Cantons were invited. Zwingli came with the Burgomaster, Diethelm Röust. Here (January 6, 1528) ten Theses, drawn up by Zwingli, Haller, and Roll, were debated. They treated of the Mass as a sacrifice, of pictures, and of Purgatory; the validity of Church ordinances, except when grounded upon God's Word, was denied. Thesis IV, "that the body and blood of Christ are substantially and corporally received in the Eucharist cannot be proved from the Scripture," caused much discussion. The Disputations ended as Zwingli wished. The Mass was replaced by sermons; images were soon removed, and even the Minster organ was broken up (February 17, 1528). In some respects, however, Bern did not follow Zurich; when the latter supported by force the Reformation in the Thurgau, Bern parted company, and her constant fear of Savoy led her to look more to the west and less to the east than did Zurich.

The Bernese Reformation was less doctrinal than the Zurich, but the secularisation of the monasteries was a great feature in its case also

(1527); the funds so derived were devoted partly to the State, partly to replacing foreign pensions, which were now definitely renounced (February, 1528). The Bernese Oberlanders, however, had hoped to share the property of the monastery at Interlaken, and, when this was seized for the government, the inhabitants of the Haslithal rose in rebellion; some citizens of Unterwalden, believing the statement of these peasants that the Reformation was forced upon them, crossed the Brünig to their help, and it cost Bern much trouble to put down the movement so supported. This incident, for which Bern claimed compensation, was a cause of much ill-will.

About a year later (February, 1529) the Reformation was carried through at Basel, but not without tumults which drove Erasmus away to Louvain, the centre of the Counter-Reformation. Mühlhausen, Schaffhausen (where the movement was democratic), St Gallen, and the Free Bailiwicks (especially Bremgarten) followed in the same direction; while Appenzell (the outer Rhodes allowing freedom of belief, 1524) and Glarus were divided; the Graubünden—where opposition to the Bishop had long existed—allowed liberty of preaching in 1526.

But Zwingli's outlook included Germany as well as Switzerland; his doctrines, opposed to those of Luther, were here working their way inwards; and therefore the relations between Emperor and Princes greatly affected him. Constance, always hostile to the Emperor, and Lindau, controlled the Lake of Constance. In the former, Protestant views, taught by the Swabian Reformer, Ambrose Blaurer, a friend of Melanchthon, and Zurik, had such hold that the Bishop (1526) moved to Meersburg, and the Chapter to Ueberlingen. The Federal Diet (November 4, 1527) refused to admit Constance as a member; but on Christmas-day the Council of Zurich decided to conclude with Constance a religious and political League, called *das christliche Bürgerrecht*. The treaty was modelled upon that which had admitted Basel to the Confederates (June 9, 1501); it contained provisions for mutual help, mainly defensive; it allowed of extension, and indeed the conquest of lands for Constance is spoken of, a seeming reference to the Thurgau. But the peculiarity of the new Treaty lay in its being based upon theological unity—a principle which was to have a long and disastrous future in diplomacy. To Strassburg—where the preachers Capito, Bucer, and Hedio were already his friends—Zwingli sent (August, 1527) an envoy to discuss its admission to the new League; the admission of Bern, discussed at the Bern Disputation, was merely a question of time; it followed Constance (June 25, 1528). The Reformation in the Common Lands was now a pressing question, and a clause in the Treaty provided that preachers there should be protected, and no subject punished for his belief; if the majority anywhere decided for Reform, they were to be left free to carry it out. The first place to which this applied was the Toggenburg, Zwingli's old home.

Other cities quickly followed: St Gallen (November 3); Biel (January 28, 1529); Mühlhausen (February 17); Basel (March 3); and after a longer interval Schaffhausen (October 15), which had a somewhat varied religious history. Strassburg, after many proposals and discussions (due to Bern's unwillingness to pass beyond Switzerland), finally entered the League (January 5, 1530), when the danger from Austria seemed great, and Zwingli's activity, stimulated by Philip of Hesse, was almost feverish. The edifice was to be crowned by the admission of Hesse; but only Zurich, Basel, and Strassburg would consent to so risky an alliance; and in the various treaties concluded with these cities the claims of the Swiss Confederation were reserved. There were proposals for a larger league, to include Augsburg, Nürnberg, and Ulm; but the anomaly of such a formation was evident, and it could not be successfully carried into execution. The inclusion of Ulrich of Württemberg in the Christian Civic League, as proposed by Philip, was, happily, not brought about. The result of the diplomatic activity in which Zwingli had engaged under the influence of Philip of Hesse thus fell far short of its purpose.

To this new League, which made the Confederation impossible, the Catholic States replied by the "Christian Union." Austria had causes of complaint in the Waldshut incident and in the monastic secularisations. The monasteries of Stein-am-Rhein and Königsfelden, the former being under Austrian protection, and the latter an Austrian foundation, had been secularised (1524). Ferdinand protested; and reprisals followed on both sides. For its Italian policy Austria had need of Swiss support (it was hopeless, said one Austrian envoy, to hold Milan unless Switzerland were with the Emperor). At the Diet at Baden (May 28, 1528) Dr Jacob Sturzl, an envoy from Ferdinand—whose policy here agreed with the Emperor's—proposed to the Five Catholic Cantons, Luzern, Schwyz, Uri, Unterwalden, and Zug, a league with Austria, partly for defence and common religious ends. War was threatened; for, while the Imperial government was eager to attack Constance, Zurich and possibly Bern were equally bound to defend it, and also to chastise Unterwalden for violating Bernese territory.

It is impossible to follow in detail Austria's policy towards Switzerland: distinctions between the policies of Charles and Ferdinand, between the Councils at Ensisheim and Innsbruck, are easily traceable. And the chief advisers were not at one. Mark Sittich of Ems—the *Vogt* of Bregenz and the Vorarlberg—and Count Rudolf von Sulz, head of the Innsbruck Council, were for war; they were further urged on by the Bishop of Constance and the Abbot of St Gallen, who had private wrongs to redress. But the Habsburg lack of funds, and the impossibility of putting fresh taxes upon impoverished lands, made against war. The desirability of regaining the old lands of the Habsburgs was always present to their advisers; yet little could be done to compass it. On the other side the dread of such an attack from "Pharaoh" was always in the mind of Zwingli, and sometimes found violent expression. But with the lapse of time he learnt that the Emperor could not always act as he would.

After lengthy negotiations the proposals for the Christian Union were drafted in a Diet at Feldkirch (February 14, 1529), and fully agreed to at Waldshut (April 22, 1529). The old faith was to be preserved and, as in 1525, a reformation on Catholic lines was to be carried out with the advice of the spiritual rulers. The members of the Union were bound to secure for each other the right of punishing heretics. A clause of doubtful interpretation about conquests showed that the possibility of such had been considered. This Union, which made a solid wall of Catholicism between South Germany and Switzerland, was, like the Civic League, a breaking-up of the old Confederation. It also looked for an extension beyond Switzerland: at the Diet of Speier (1529) Ferdinand discussed with Bavaria and the Bishop of Salzburg their entry into the Catholic League; Savoy was spoken of as likely to join it; the Valais also had (May, 1528) contracted a league for ten years with Savoy; even the Swabian League, it was said, might become a member. Bern and Zurich would then be enclosed by enemies.

The Diet of Speier (February 21, 1529) issued a severe decree against sects denying the Sacrament of the Flesh and Blood of Christ;—a distinction, which the Protestants had not as yet formally made for themselves, was made by others. Nine of the fourteen cities that signed the Protest presented on this occasion were Zwinglian. Strassburg, which was in disgrace at the Diet for having just abolished the Mass, drew closer to Zurich, from both political and theological motives. The distinction between Lutherans and Zwinglians on the subject of the Eucharist became now of political as well as dogmatic importance.

Events were tending towards war in Switzerland. Bern and Zurich had agreed (November 16-18, 1528) both to compel Unterwalden to pay the indemnity for invading Bernese territory, and also to protect the Reformed faith in the Common Lands, while the several communities were to be left free to decide for the Reformed or Catholic side. At a meeting of the Thurgau *Landsgemeinde* at Weinfelden (December 9, 1528) envoys of both the Catholic and Reformed Cantons attended; the latter promised help to those upon their side, and asked their help in return. The majority of the Thurgau communities decided for Reform. Meanwhile, the difficulties of a divided government in the Common Territories had become increasingly acute. Moreover, to the west, Geneva was attacked by Savoy, to which the Valais—now (end of 1528) allied to the Five Cantons—was attached, and the Christian Union supported Savoy. As these alliances tended to war, Schaffhausen, Appenzell, and the Graubünden offered mediation. But, as their terms did not include freedom of preaching, Zurich—firm on this point—

would not listen to them. Of the Five Cantons, Unterwalden was now the bitterest; but Luzern and Zurich—the rival leaders—had made up their mind for war (May 26-28). Bern, anxious to preserve unity, would not promise Zurich help for an offensive war. The demands of Zurich were indeed excessive; the surrender of the rights of the Cantons to the administration of the Abbey of St Gallen (to which Zurich, Luzern, Schwyz, and Glarus sent a protecting bailiff in turn every two years), the withdrawal from the Austrian alliance, and the surrender of the Luzern satirist, Thomas Murner.

Riotous proceedings at St Gallen were a further cause of war. In 1528 it was Zurich's turn to appoint the bailiff, who both attended to secular business and protected the Abbey; Zwingli meant to use the opportunity to further his cause. The Abbot Franz Geissberger was dying; Zwingli and the Privy Council bade (January 28, 1529) the Zurich official (Jacob Frei) seize the monastic property upon his death, secularise it, and introduce the Gospel. But the townsmen broke into the abbey (February 23) before the death of Geissberger (March 23). The monks elected as Abbot Kilian Käuffi, who fled to Bregenz, and thence resisted the plunder of his abbey lands. Since the abbey was under the protection of the Empire as well as of the four Cantons, and of these Luzern and Schwyz supported Käuffi, the illegal action of Zurich and of the townsmen could not but lead to war.

Nor did this incident stand alone: the delicate constitutional question of the Free Bailiwicks added to the intensity of feeling. Nearly all the villages in the district had declared (May, 1529) that they would follow Zurich, which was openly encouraging their violent changes; in all but religion they would obey their lords, the Catholic majority of the Cantons. These lords, however, hesitated to use force; but embassies regained for Catholicism some parishes. A new bailiff sent by Unterwalden was to take office in May (1529), and at first Zurich resolved to prevent his entry.

Bern did its utmost to keep the peace, but Zurich was embittered, while the Five Cantons had enough cause to reject Bern's mediation. Zurich declared war (June 8), and carried out a plan of campaign which Zwingli had drawn up; leaving small detachments at Muri and elsewhere, near the Bernese troops at Bremgarten (for Bern, which disliked offensive war, was yet willing to defend the Common Lands and Zurich if attacked), the main body moved to Kappel, ten miles from Zurich. Zwingli's plan was to move suddenly against the enemy; to force them to give up the Austrian alliance and their rule in the Common Lands, to renounce pensions, and to allow free preaching in their own territory. The Five Cantons, hoping to the last for Austrian help, were badly prepared: the troops of Luzern had gone to the Free Bailiwicks, but those of the other four Cantons moved from Zug towards Zurich. Hans Oebli, the *Landammann* of Glarus, hurried up to mediate; and, as he was a friend of Reform,

CH. X.

his voice, in spite of Zwingli's plea for war, prevailed. The rank and file of neither army wished for war; and so, by the help of other Cantons, peace was negotiated by ambassadors, first at Aarau and then at Steinhausen in Zug; the decision lay by custom with the armies themselves. Zwingli wished to force the abolition of pensions upon his opponents, but even at Zurich some were against this, and Bern, through Nicholas Manuel, refused to enforce it. Finally (June 24, 1529) peace was made at Kappel. Neither party was to attack the other for its faith. In the Common Lands, the religious offenders should not be punished; the majority were to decide for or against the Mass and on other questions; only men of honour and moderation should be sent there as bailiffs. The Austrian alliance was renounced, and its very documents were cut into shreds and burnt; the Five Cantons were to pay a war indemnity according to the decision of arbitrators, and, if it remained unpaid, Zurich and Bern might close their markets to the Five Cantons. Finally the abolition of pensions and mercenary service was recommended to the Five Cantons. The removal of the Austrian alliance seemed to secure the advantage to Zurich, which still kept Hesse and its chance of France. One clause was afterwards differently construed; it ran, that as faith cannot be planted by force no coercion should be used against the Five Cantons or their people in matters touching their faith. The Zwinglians thought that free preaching extended to the Five Cantons as well as to the Common Lands; and on the other hand the Five Cantons naturally held themselves free to act as they pleased in their own territory. Thus the peace which placed Zurich at the height of her power contained in itself the seeds of future war. As a politician, if not as a theologian, Zwingli was justified in his preference for force. As early as August he thought another campaign inevitable.

In this same year the question of the Eucharist became of crucial importance for the Protestants. In his writings of 1522 Zwingli had entered into no criticism of the accepted view. The interpretation, in our Lord's saying, "This is my body," of the word "is" as "signifies" was possibly suggested to him by Cornelius van Hoen, after 1521, in a circular letter carried about to theologians by Henne Rode. The expression of his opinion was hastened, if not caused, by Carlstadt's extreme utterances, containing (as Zwingli thought) a kernel of truth hidden by errors, and it first took shape in a letter to Matthäus Alber of Reutlingen (November 16, 1524): the Eucharist was regarded as purely symbolical, but as a pledge of Christian profession; and he emphasised, as his controversy with the Anabaptists shows, the corporate aspect in the Eucharist.

Zwingli's teaching, often presented as a mere negation of Luther's, was no less a negation of the doctrine of the Church. In spite of varying views as to the exact nature of the Presence, its reality had always been admitted: Wiclif's denial of Transubstantiation and Luther's

The question of the Eucharist. Marburg Conference. 29

assertion of Consubstantiation, although affecting the relation of the Presence to the elements, had not called in question that reality or the supernatural grace of this Sacrament itself. Zwingli, fastening upon the direct relation between God and the individual apart from outward acts, and starting from the human side, made this Sacrament purely symbolical, and brought it down from the supernatural to the human plane. In this he was followed by the later Sacramentarians, and was at one with the Socinians and more radical sects. He thus became the revolutionary theologian of the Reformation. While the Lutherans were sensitive to charges of a departure from the Catholic faith, the Zwinglians were conscious of their own bold innovations in doctrine and organisation (for instance, they did not hold Ordination essential). Their divergence from the Catholic Church went far deeper than objections to the Papacy or to current abuses; and thus the vision of a Council to promote union had no attraction or possibility for them. Hence the growth of their influence tended to perpetuate disunion.

The south German cities were led to favour Zwingli's views, not only from democratic sympathy with the Swiss, but from dislike of Luther's political allies, the Princes. Nürnberg was an exception: in 1525 Zwingli's books were forbidden there as "books of the Devil." But by April, 1527, most of the Augsburg preachers were on his side; at Ulm Conrad Sam was a pillar of strength to him; Ulrich of Württemberg, influenced by Œcolampadius and then by Zwingli's sermons (1524-5), became a strong Zwinglian, and in Hesse influenced the Landgrave in his turn; at Mainz, Hedio, who came from Basel (1523) corresponded with Zwingli; Frankfort, through Froschauer's connexion, became a literary centre of the "pure doctrine"; Strassburg, inspired by Zwingli, sent out its own teachers; and Zwinglianism, spreading down the Rhine, met a similar current of doctrine originating with van Hoen in Holland; it reached even Friesland, where Carl Stadt had worked, and Luther, unable to understand such a rapid growth, ascribed it to the Devil.

Haner, a theologian who differed from Luther in maintaining a purely spiritual eating and drinking of the Saviour's flesh and blood, and from Zwingli in maintaining a supernatural communication of grace, had suggested to the Landgrave Philip the possibility of a conference clearing up all differences. This advice, given at Speier in 1529, where unity among the Protestants was desirable for both political and religious reasons, led to the Marburg Conference (September, 1529). The character and issue of this Conference have been described elsewhere. The central subject was the change wrought by consecration in the elements. Zwingli purposely restricted the discussion to leave hope for unity; he had a practical mind, accustomed more than Luther's to the give and take of equal discussion. So long as unity was based upon ecclesiastical organisation, there had been scope for difference of opinion within one

Church; but now, when organic unity was lost, exact agreement of theological opinion and the names of certain leaders were made the essentials of the unity which it was sought to secure. Luther was the obstacle, as insisting that union of any kind should depend upon absolute agreement. But it is hard to see how Luther could have come into union with Zwingli, without joining in his political schemes; since the demand for a union between them was primarily political.

The failure to achieve theological unity ruined the great plan for a league which Zwingli and Philip of Hesse had conceived. Jacob Meier of Basel had spoken of some considerable plan to be discussed at Marburg; Zwingli's correspondence with the Landgrave and his visit to Strassburg had suggested many things to him; his request for an official delegate from the Zurich Council did not aim at theology alone. Unfortunately, the invitation to Bern was not sent until September 10, when it was too late. Religious differences made it clear that Saxony and Switzerland could not be included in the same league. However, Philip was ready to do without Saxony, and he was also ready to seek help from France, —an expedient which loyalty to the Empire made distasteful to Saxony. The proposal of such a plan came from Philip; the exact details were afterwards filled in by Zwingli, inspired from Strassburg. Not only France but Venice was to be drawn into the league; and the instructions to Collin, the envoy there, were drawn up by Zwingli himself, as were many other State papers.

The activity and the expenditure of the French agents (Boisregault and Meigret) in Switzerland were great; the Most Christian King had no scruple about negotiations with heretics (who indeed were better than Turks); in March, 1531, he was ready to help Zurich secretly. But his great object was to keep the balance even in Switzerland; a war was not in his interest. On the other hand, the fear of arousing France paralysed the Emperor's action. Hence, while foreign influences pushed Switzerland to the verge of war, they also served to keep it back from war itself.

Diplomacy took up much of Zwingli's time, but his pen was as active as ever: he wrote commentaries upon Isaiah and Jeremiah, a number of important letters, and controversial tracts. His power at Zurich and the spirit of the city were at their height. In a complaint to Luzern about Thomas Murner (whose *Heretics' Calendar* seemed dangerous and offensive to an age over-sensitive to ridicule) the Council said (February 14, 1529) that they were free, and subject to no Emperor or lord; they, like France, Venice, and other States, ordered spiritual persons and property as they thought well. Zwingli's enemies too were now under his feet; after December 7, 1528, only the barest civic rights without the chance of office were left to non-Reformers; attendance at Mass even outside the city was punished by fine; to eat fish instead of flesh on Friday was an offence. But a reaction might at any time set in.

It was indeed the fear of such a reaction that led Zwingli to make his Reformation as thorough as possible.

In this period it becomes impossible to separate Swiss politics from German. The restoration of Duke Ulrich of Württemberg (which Zurich was more disposed than Bern to help) was an unfailing subject of negotiation. With this Saul who, could he but be restored, seemed likely to be a Paul to the Reformation, Zwingli had a connexion of long standing; and through him he became friendly with that able politician, the Landgrave Philip of Hesse. Zwingli's Hessian correspondence in cipher begins with the second Diet of Speier, when the Landgrave (April 22, 1529) first wrote about the Marburg Conference, and it ends eleven days before Zwingli's death. The two correspondents formed vast schemes, for the Landgrave, like Zwingli himself, was no rigid conservative. As early as 1524 Zwingli had formed a plan for an extensive league; but the Anabaptist troubles led him to lay it aside. Now under the Landgrave's influence he returned to it. After the Conference the proposal of "a Christian agreement" came from Hesse; it aimed at securing mutual protection and converts to the Word of God; the Schmalkaldic League (April, 1531) owed something to this conception. But the idea of a league uniting Swiss and German Protestants failed through resistance from the Elector of Saxony, faithful to the Empire and firm in his Lutheran creed.

The reward Zwingli gained for deserting his old principle of keeping aloof from foreign complications was small; his widest plans miscarried. No greater success rewarded Bucer in his attempts at mediation between the Lutheran and Zwinglian camps. The creed of Strassburg, Constance, Memmingen, and Lindau, drawn up by Bucer and Capito, presented to the Emperor July 11, 1530, and known as the *Tetrapolitana*, was considered and rejected by Basel and Zurich at the Evangelic Diet of Basel, November 16, 1530. It affirmed that the true body and blood of Christ were given, truly to eat and drink, for the nourishment of souls; positively, it made as close an approach to the Lutheran view as was possible, while by omission of any statement as to the elements it avoided contradicting that view; in other articles the authority of the Scriptures, not mentioned in the Augsburg Confession, and the rejection of images are set forth. Zwingli's own Confession was embodied in the *Fidei ratio ad Carolum Imperatorem* presented to the Emperor (July 3, 1530). The earlier sections expounded the Nicene faith; the sixth section emphasized Wyclif's theory of the invisible Church composed of elect believers; the seventh and eighth asserted the Sacraments to be merely signs and affirmed Zwingli's teaching in terms likely to anger Catholics and Lutherans alike; later sections depreciated ceremonies, denounced images as unscriptural, magnified the office of preacher, and discussed the relations of Church and State at length. The Anabaptists were often incidentally condemned, and the assertion of his own views was clear and unflinching. No wish to conciliate others, no fear of a breach with the past is apparent.

Even when Strassburg (December, 1530) joined the Schmalkaldic League, Zwingli's desire for political union did not overcome his conscientious adherence to his own views. He was thus the obstacle in the negotiations at this stage (March–July, 1531), when the Elector of Saxony had yielded so far as to admit the adherents of the *Tetrapolitana* to the Schmalkaldic League. While he was willing to leave something vague, he could not accept definitions which he held to be untrue. Moreover, the Lutherans desired a General Council; while Zwingli had completely broken with tradition, and his organisation left no room for Councils.

Apart from doctrine, Zwinglianism on its political side was now (1530–1) a greater danger to the Empire than was Lutheranism. Ferdinand wrote to the Emperor after the battle of Kappel, that Switzerland was the head of German Protestantism, and to conquer it was the true way of mastering Germany and re-establishing religious peace; the papal Legate at Brussels wrote to Clement VII (May, 1531); "*Zurich est désormais la tête et la capitale de la secte Luthérienne.*" But her power was declining. It was only a small gain that Ulm (July, 1531), moved by the definite refusal of Electoral Saxony to alter its position, became more Zwinglian, or that Bern, whose support was essential to Zurich, rejected the *Tetrapolitana*. In Zurich itself Zwingli's influence was lessening; the unrestrained power of the Privy Council had grown distasteful, and the disaffected nobility was regaining power; on the question of an embassy to France (February, 1531), the opposition showed itself stronger than his followers. The trade of the city had been injured by political unrest; strict sumptuary laws and moral control led to discontent among the artisans and tradesmen, who regretted the monasteries; the sermons lost some of their old attraction. So keenly did Zwingli feel this change, that he formally asked leave to resign his preachership and go to work elsewhere (July 26). But he was too closely bound up with the town, and at the prayer of a deputation, made up of the two Burgomasters and the three chief Gild-masters, he kept his office; and for the last months of his life he retained, though precariously, something of his former influence.

Inside the Confederation war was again drawing nearer; the Catholic Cantons had still their own grievances and were embittered by defeat: they still—although against hope—looked to Austria for help. Zwingli, angry at the insults to which he was subjected, was decidedly for war ("The knot can only be loosed by firmness"). In this state of affairs the war of Musso kindled the flame. The castellan of Musso (di Medigino), since 1525 a troublesome neighbour of the Graubünden, had (March, 1531) murdered a Graubünden envoy returning from Milan, and invaded the Valtelline. The League appealed to the Swiss and especially to Zurich. Zwingli believed that the Emperor stood behind the castellan, and that movements of troops in Austria foreshadowed an attack upon Zurich—an event which German politics made not unlikely. The Emperor did not indeed himself support the castellan, but he was inclined to approve the war, since it kept the dangerous Swiss employed, and he was not unwilling that Musso should be helped without expense to himself lest, if left without help, the castellan should turn to France. The Swiss Diet was divided by the Graubünden request. The Five Cantons refused help: the Protestants promised it. Zwingli again, in the Privy Council and in closest touch with the French ambassador Meigret, seized the opportunity to revive his far-reaching plan of alliance.

Political means were used for religious objects. An assembly of the Zwinglian allies (May 15) at Zurich determined that the Five Cantons must be forced to allow free way to preaching. An embargo upon trade by land—to check the passage of wine, wheat, salt, and iron—was to be set up against the Five Cantons. It was an unhappy method of compulsion, although it had a precedent in 1438, and had been contemplated in the First Peace of Kappel. The chief responsibility belongs to Bern, who suggested it as an alternative to the war proposed by Zurich. Things drifted nearer to war in spite of representations from France and from the other Cantons: scarcity of food distressed and angered the Catholics; Zurich would only remove the embargo if free preaching were allowed.

The Forest Cantons this time made the first move, and from Zug marched towards Zurich (October 4-9). When news of this reached Zurich, a small band, which in the end reached 1200, under George Göldli set out (October 9); a larger band of 1500 men fairly well equipped started two days later, and Zwingli accompanied them. But there was a lack of enthusiasm and even of preparation. In Bern the people blamed Zwingli for this "parsons' war." The action of Bern indeed was ambiguous; partly owing to trouble nearer home, and partly from aversion to the war. Her contingent was not ready until the crisis had passed. But there is no need to look for open treachery when a house is divided against itself.

The advance guard under Göldli—which was only to keep on the defensive—began the battle at Kappel on October 11; they neglected to charge the enemy when changing their attack, and their position was turned. When the main body under Rudolf Lavater reached the Albis —the position fixed by the Council—the day was practically lost. Its attack upon the 8000 Forest men failed. Zwingli was among the slain, and his body was treated disgracefully as that of a traitor. His stepson, Gerold Meyer, Diebold von Geroldscok, Abbot Joner of Kappel, and others of his friends, perished with him.

The remaining Zurich troops and allies came up (October 24) with the Catholic troops on the Gubel near Zug and were defeated in an engagement more serious than the first. Zurich lay open to its enemies: the Emperor might now have intervened with effect. But through the mediation of the French ambassadors and the other Cantons peace was made (November 23): the conditions of the First Peace of Kappel were now reversed. It was to the credit of the victors that they did not press their success too far. Even now Zurich was not disposed for peace; but the country villages, which had lost by the embargo, here as at Bern were strongly for it. By the Second Peace of Kappel the territory of Zurich was kept intact: in the Common Lands existing beliefs were left alone, but Catholic minorities, where there were such, received protection; government by the majority of the Cantons was affirmed. The management of its own religious matters was left to each Canton. Zwingli's scheme to force the Catholic Cantons to give free play to the Reformation in the Common Lands and in their own territory had failed; but the principle of Federal control over religion was not asserted. The Christian Civic Alliance and the Treaty of 1529 were annulled. Basel, Schaffhausen, St Gallen, and Mühlhausen paid indemnities of from 1000 to 4000 crowns. Zurich and the town of St Gallen were to compensate and restore the Abbey of St Gallen: the Reformed communities in the Free Bailiwicks, Thurgau, and Toggenburg (where the Abbot regained his power), were allowed to keep their faith; Catholic, but not Reformed, minorities were protected. Monks and nuns might return to their Houses. Solothurn restored its old worship to escape the payment of an indemnity. Bern, which had to forego the compensation from Unterwalden, and Zurich were left discontented and almost bankrupt. Zurich was forced (December, 1531) to grant the Kappel Charter, by which its rural districts gained a right to be consulted upon all important questions, and to give or refuse their consent for any future war. Such was the outcome of Zwingli's ambitious scheme, whereby Bern and Zurich were to be the pillars of a great Protestant power in Switzerland, extending its influence far afield. The peace perpetuated division among the Reformers, and separated Switzerland from Germany. Glarus became Catholic once more; Bern grew more Lutheran; in the Common Lands the Aargau suffered most reaction, the Thurgau least. Zurich is henceforth externally of less importance. The future of Swiss Protestantism lay with Bern and Geneva, the latter not yet a Confederate, but in league with Bern and Freiburg (February, 1528).

And, furthermore, the Counter-Reformation, or the Catholic Reaction, (neither name aptly describes the movement or its origin) found a ready home in Switzerland. Catholicism began to gain ground here soon after the Second Treaty of Kappel, without having to wait for any of the stimulating movements felt elsewhere; the scheme of Catholic reform proposed in 1524–5, and the disasters of Zwinglianism were effective local causes.

Outside Powers were unwilling to let the war die out; Philip of

Hesse, always ready and hopeful, tried to rouse it to new life, Basel was arming, but the south German towns urged peace. The Pope called upon the Emperor to make an end and put down the heresy at once, and even sent to the Five Cantons "*aliquantum pecuniae*": Ferdinand would have done the same, but was overruled by his advisers. The Austrian statesmen hoped to use the war for the Emperor's good, but to do so without expense: and the Emperor feared by any decisive step to rouse the French to war. The French on their part gained greatly by the Peace. Thus the settlement remained undisturbed, and the south German towns drew nearer to the Princes now that Zurich could give them no help.

In Zurich itself the religious movement continued: Bullinger, Zwingli's son-in-law and successor, banished from Bremgarten by the Peace, carried on his work; but it was now solely theological and internal; the Privy Council was discredited, as Bullinger explained to Myconius. Its existence meant foreign entanglements. And Zurich, weakened by the new power given to the country districts, became less and less able to pursue an adventurous foreign policy among the great States of Europe.

But the strife of doctrine remained behind, always significant for the history of thought, at times for politics as well. Bucer's task of mediation grew harder and its end more remote. Conferences with Melanchthon had no result, because it was impossible to devise a formula such as would satisfy Luther and still recognise the conflicting doctrines adapted to minds of different types. At Wittenberg (May 22–27, 1536) a well-attended Conference produced a conciliatory document, the *Wittenberg Concord*. According to it, the body and blood of Christ were truly and substantially present in the Eucharist, shown and received. Bucer, by a distinction not widely accepted, contended that the impious did not, while the merely unworthy did, receive them. To this view Strassburg, Augsburg, Ulm, Constance, and other cities agreed. But Luther hesitated to sign the Concord because he heard the Swiss had agreed to it, and feared it must therefore be bad.

On the other hand, in the previous January, the Swiss theologians had met at Basel and there drawn up the First Helvetic Confession. It was conciliatory in tone, and went beyond the purely symbolic view, the *nuda signa*, of Zwingli. But its framers were not at Wittenberg; and Bucer, the medium of intercourse, did not adequately represent one side to the other. Another Conference of the Swiss Reformers at Basel drafted a new document, showing a wish for unity, and at the same time making it clear why the Wittenberg Concord could not possibly be accepted. Luther's reply (1537) was guarded and distrustful, so that its circulation in Switzerland did not help the cause which Bucer and Melanchthon had at heart. A Conference at Zurich (April 28, 1538) showed the politicians as eager for unity as the theologians for distinction. Finally, Zurich (September 28, 1538) resolved to keep to her old view with no modifications. If doctrine was to be the basis of unity, the adjustment of the limits of difference required nice discussion. Luther's violence of language, and Zwingli's mingling of politics and theology, had complicated that discussion; henceforth, old positions eagerly guarded and attacked, associations and repugnances valued above their real importance, were further obstacles to union. But it was hard to give any strong religious reasons why unity as distinct from charity should be sought. Political reasons there were in plenty, but their admission made the discussions theologically lifeless.

Calvin may have learnt much of organisation from Zurich; but in theological importance he overshadows not only Zwingli but all other Swiss reformers. As to the Eucharist, while Zwinglian in his exegesis he was more spiritual in his conceptions, emphasising the grace conferred, while not connecting it with the elements; a change which has also been detected in Bullinger and later Zwinglians. But they agreed in rejecting Luther's doctrine. Like Bucer Calvin worked for unity, and unlike Zwingli did not spread his political energies over too large a field. He was thus able to concentrate and deepen influences set in motion by Zwingli. But even Calvin's labours for unity had a political end: if to observers from the outside German and French Protestants could appear united, the French King, ally of the one, could not well persecute the other. Calvin and Bullinger drew up (1549) the *Consensus Tigurinus*—strongly anti-Lutheran in tone (*perversa et impia superstitio est ipsum Christum sub elementis includere*). Up to this time there had been a division among the Swiss leaders: Bullinger had given up all hope of unity with the Lutherans: at Bern, with its Lutheran inclinations, that hope was still alive. But with the *Consensus* Protestant Switzerland was united. Basel, with traditions of synods of its own, Bern, while seeing no need for the issue of a fresh formula, agreed with its doctrine; Schaffhausen, St Gallen, Biel, and Mühlhausen joined in accepting it. The Second Helvetic Confession (1562-6) united all but Basel, which only subscribed to it eighty years later. Thus in the end dogmatic and political unity— which had so often helped or thwarted each other—claimed a common territory in Reformed Switzerland. And the reaction following upon Zwingli's strict control brought a growth of toleration. In Germany, meanwhile, the teaching of Zwingli became nominally less important than that of Calvin, and the division between Reformed and Lutheran— so fatal to German Protestantism—belongs in its later stages more to the history of Calvinism than of Zwinglianism. But Zwingli in his treatment of the Eucharist had raised a fundamental issue; and his views on this head, like his treatment of public worship, have had a wider influence than their recognition in Confessions and Liturgies would indicate. Thus Zwinglianism became the name of a school of thought rather than of a religious body.

Zwingli's plans would have given the Confederation unity and cohesion at the expense of his opponents. But the Reformation postponed the solution of the unsolved problem of Swiss unity; and the Counter-Reformation made the difficulties greater. Cardinal Carlo Borromeo, Archbishop of Milan, took a deep interest in Switzerland: he founded a Swiss College at Milan, introduced into the land the Jesuits (1574-81) and the Capuchins (1581-8), and procured a permanent nunciature at Luzern. After his death Luzern, under Ludwig Pfyffer, formed a league with Uri, Schwyz, Unterwalden, Zug, Solothurn, and Freiburg to maintain offensively and defensively the Catholic Faith (1586): this was known as the Borromean League. Thus the division into two camps was crystallised, and the old Federal Constitution was almost dissolved: Diets—save those of the opposed Cantons held separately—became rare. The disputes about the Common Lands went on and with foreign influences intensified the differences due to faith. In the Thirty Years' War the Protestants expressly and the Catholics tacitly adopted neutrality, but could not hold entirely aloof. The country's importance to its neighbours lay in its provision of soldiers for hire, and for this reason they endured its independence. The neutrality adopted was not that advocated yet departed from by Zwingli: it resulted from the religious divisions due to him, combined with the foreign service he condemned.

The Reformation in Switzerland shows how largely the forms in which religious ideas express themselves are moulded by political forces. It was also more than elsewhere the centre of the national history. It was Zwingli who, by his religious influence, and his political mistakes, was the cause of this. Politically his dearest schemes miscarried; ecclesiastically his type of organisation and worship endured; doctrinally he was overshadowed by others. But the permanent division of the Cantons was due to him: not merely to the doctrines he taught, but on the one hand to the power with which he impressed them upon Zurich, and on the other, to the energy and violence with which, regardless of Federal liberties, he strove to force them upon the other Cantons.

www.ingramcontent.com/pod-product-compliance
Lightning Source LLC
Chambersburg PA
CBHW061311040426
42444CB00010B/2591